BIRDS OF THE WORLD
WADING BIRDS

BIRDS OF THE WORLD
WADING BIRDS

JOHN P.S. MACKENZIE

SWAN·HILL
PRESS

Design: First Image
Typesetting: First Image
Printed and bound in Hong Kong by Book Art Inc., Toronto

Swan Hill Press
An Imprint of Airlife Publishing Ltd
101 Longden Road, Shrewsbury SY3 9EB, England

Page 2: Great Blue Heron (*Ardea herodias*)   Four feet tall, the Great Blue is the
American counterpart of the Gray Heron of Europe, Africa and Asia. It nests
in colonies high in trees through most of North America, and winters to
northern South America. An all-white form is found in southern Florida.

Pages 4-5: Chilean Flamingo (*Phoenicopterus chilensis*)   This species is more
widely spread than the Andean or Puna Flamingos for it lives from the salt
lakes of the highlands to the brackish estuaries and coastal marshes. Its
range extends from Chile to Paraguay, Uruguay and Brazil. A few have
strayed as far south as the Falkland Islands.

CONTENTS

INTRODUCTION

Left: Long-billed Dowitcher (*Limnodromus scolopaceus*)   The Long-billed and Short-billed Dowitchers are extremely similar in appearance, although their calls differ. This one gives a sharp *keek* cry. It nests at the limits of land in Alaska, Canada, and Siberia, and migrates as far as Argentina. When feeding they plunge their long bills into the soft mud with an action resembling that of a sewing machine.

Chinese Egret (*Egretta eulophotes*)   This handsome egret is displaying its nuptial plumes. Its yellow bill and toes are diagnostic, as is the blue facial patch in front of the eye. It nests in trees, principally in eastern China, and migrates to south eastern Asia and Indonesia, appearing periodically in northern Australia. It feeds inland in rice fields, ponds and streams.

Feeding habitats for the nearly 9,000 bird species in the world include virtually every place that food can be found, and the range of food taken includes almost everything that grows that is not too big to be swallowed. Birds feed in the air, on the land, and in the water — eating all manner of vegetable and animal matter. We shall consider here those families of birds that feed, either principally or exclusively, at the margins of water, fresh and salt, and in the marshes. What is particular to them is that they take some or all of their food in shallow water while wading. They include the herons, ibises, flamingos, cranes, jacanas, oystercatchers, plovers, sandpipers, avocets, stilts, storks, and rails. Other birds are associated with water margins in their feeding — ducks and geese for instance — but they are excluded because they feed principally while swimming, upending and taking food from the bottom. Red-winged Blackbirds, which use a marshy habitat for nesting and feeding, are primarily land birds. Many of the 91 species of kingfishers take their food from the water, but they do so by diving from the air and observing their prey from prominent perches. A large portion of the kingfisher species, however, feeds on insects and small vertebrates, which they find in the forests well away from water.

Many of the wading birds are migratory, travelling north or south to nest and reversing direction before the onset of winter when food supplies dwindle and the water freezes. The most extensive travellers are some of the plovers and sandpipers. Several species of these birds travel from Cape Horn to the Arctic in spring and by July start the return journey. The White-rumped Sandpiper has, next to the Arctic Tern, the world's longest migration route, from southern Ellesmere Island to Tierra del Fuego — some 9,000 miles each way. Other species that nest in warm areas may migrate only short distances or not at all. Examples are the jacanas, which live in sub-tropical areas, and some of the rails.

Wading birds feed primarily on animal matter — fish, crustacea, worms, insects, larvae, and plankton, which they capture on or near the surface of the water or by probing with their bills into the mud. However, most are quite capable of remaining healthy for long periods on a diet of vegetable matter. Some plovers and sandpipers arrive at the nesting grounds before the thaw has released their usual food, and sustain themselves on berries from the previous season. Those species that make long non-stop flights over the ocean pause for a week or so on the Labrador or adjacent coasts and feed on crowberries, thus building up fat and stored energy for the long and perilous journey.

The physical features and feeding behaviors of birds have evolved together to fit each to a particular way of life. Thus, bill size and shape and the length of the necks and legs are important in determining food selection. The strong conical bills of finches and parrots are suitable for crushing seeds; the hooked bills of raptors for tearing flesh. Most waders have relatively long legs and necks for wading and running and thin pointed bills suitable for probing. Some, like the plovers, have relatively short blunt bills, for they feed while running about snapping up larvae and other matter at the margins of water.

American Bittern (*Botaurus lentiginosus*)   Known in the vernacular as the "stake driver," the bittern usually calls at dusk, with a sound similar to driving a pile into soft mud with a mallet. Preferring fresh water marshes, it nests through most of Canada and Mexico. It is a skulker, difficult to spot against the marsh reeds.

HERONS AND BITTERNS

Green-backed Heron (*Butorides striatus*)   This heron is distributed worldwide (with the exception of Europe), wherever it can find shallow water on ponds, marshes, riverbanks or mangroves in which to catch small fish, insects, and frogs. At night it even feeds on urban and suburban lawns. In North America it is rare north of the U.S. border with Canada.

When I was a boy people were convinced that the enormous blue-gray birds that stalked the edge of the marsh below our New Brunswick cottage all summer were cranes, and so they appeared to me for several years. They stood four feet tall with very long legs and sinuous necks, waiting for the small fish of the tidal pond to come within range. Occasionally the S-shaped neck would straighten suddenly as the long bill flashed into the shallow water. Usually there would be a wriggling fish grasped at its tip. Sometimes the prey would be quite large, requiring the bird to manipulate it into a suitable position for swallowing. Then one could see the neck swell as the fish was forced down its long passage. This was, of course, the Great Blue Heron, and not a crane at all.

On impulse, or when disturbed, these great birds would lift themselves into the air on broad wings that spanned six feet, to fly on slow beats to another site. In flight Great Blue Herons, like others of their family, trail their long spindly-looking legs behind them with their necks curled back, their head against their shoulders.

Herons are colonial birds, making large stick nests in tall trees, sometimes in groups of up to fifty birds. We discovered the colony of the birds that we watched some four miles inland in mixed forest. It is not unusual for the members of a heron colony to spread out over a large number of fishing places ten miles or more from the colony.

Our marsh in New Brunswick was full of birds. Another that we saw daily was known to us as the Marsh Hen or, in vernacular terms, as thunder-pump or stake-driver. This was the American Bittern, which derived its local names from its remarkable call, most often heard at dusk — a far-carrying *oonk-a-lunk* similar to the sound of driving a stake into the mud with a wooden mallet. The bittern is noted for its habit of standing motionless with its bill pointed skyward at the approach of an intruder, its eyes being so placed that it can then see in front. American Bitterns are a rich brown with streaked underparts, so that they are difficult to find against a barrier of reeds at the pond edge.

Bitterns nest on the ground, either in the reeds and cattails of the marsh or in adjacent fields. Many bird species lay their full clutch of eggs (three to six for bitterns) before commencing to incubate. This results in all the young hatching within a day. Bitterns start to incubate as soon as the first egg is laid, giving advantage to the earliest hatchlings. It is seldom that all the chicks survive the competition of the older siblings.

Herons and bitterns, of which there are 67 species, live throughout the temperate world. The heron tribe includes the egrets and the night herons, which have shorter necks and heavier bills. Night herons, as the name implies, become active at dusk, spending the day perched conspicuously in large trees.

While the Great Blue Heron is the best known of the marsh birds in North America, its counterpart in Europe is the Gray Heron, equal in size and similar in shape and habits. It too has a long black plume on the head during nesting season. It has a white neck with a tracery of black down the front and a gray mantle. The Gray Heron nests as far north as southern Scandinavia and withdraws to southern Europe and Africa during the winter. Remarkably, there is a permanent population in southern Iceland.

All birds preen to maintain clean healthy feathers, most using oil from glands near the tail. Herons are unusual in that they have a set of feathers that crumble to a powder — this is then applied to the other feathers.

The Little Blue Heron of North and South America is, as an adult, uniformly slate-blue, but as an immature is white, closely resembling the immature Snowy Egret. The breeding range in the east extends north to Maine but, curiously, young birds wander northeast into Atlantic Canada in late summer.

Among the herons, the egrets are an attractive group of medium-sized birds, most having white plumage. An exception is the handsome Reddish Egret, which has a dark blue body with pale plumes on the back and a shaggy rufous head and neck during the breeding season. This bird is noted for "mantling" — spreading its wings while standing in the water. This creates a shadow that fish mistake for protection, usually to their sorrow.

Egrets, particularly the Snowy Egret, provided plumes for ladies' hats and shawls until well into the twentieth century. The millinery trade was responsible for the near extinction of the Snowy Egret and, indirectly, for the creation of the National Audubon Society and the early legislation protecting North American birds. Recovery was, for a time, substantial, but loss of habitat in nesting areas, occasional hurricanes and human pressures have reduced breeding possibilities for these and other marsh species.

The Cattle Egret is traditionally widespread throughout Africa and Asia. During the last half century it has extended its range in southern Europe and, at about the same time, arrived in Australia and, somewhat later, in New Zealand. Earlier it had appeared in Surinam and Brazil. Here it found a suitable habitat, and has prospered in the Americas. Clearing, and the extension of cattle-grazing, provided the impetus for expansion of the bird's range through Central America to the United States, and even into southern Canada. It is now present in almost every field in the sub-tropical areas where there are hoofed animals, and is often found perched on the backs of animals that attract flies and other insects. It wanders close to the feet of grazing cattle, snapping up the insects that they disturb. These smallish egrets, standing some 20 inches high and with a three-foot wingspan, nest in large colonies in bushes and trees and sometimes on the ground. They are white with a yellow bill and legs, but in the breeding season develop a fawn-colored crest, chest and back patches; the bill then turns bright red and the legs dusky-red.

In most countries the impact of herons on fish stocks is negligible and usually beneficial, for they commonly feed on coarse fish, which are the easiest to catch. In England and Europe, however, the Gray Heron quickly reacted to the development of fish farms by using them as a source of food. Fish farmers defended their crops and during the 1970s some 5,000 Gray Herons were shot in England alone each year, reducing the population to about 10,000 birds. Remedial measures to protect the fish by means other than shooting have led to a partial recovery.

Yellow-crowned Night Heron (*Nyctanassa violacea*) Here we see an adult bird in breeding plumage, with a strongly colored yellow crown. It appears sparingly to New England, but is more common south to Brazil. It prefers salt and brackish water habitats and is more active by day than the Black-crowned Night Heron.

Goliath Heron (*Ardea goliath*)   One of the largest of the herons, the Goliath stands nearly five feet tall. It is uncommon and resides in the eastern part of Africa from Ethiopia to Tanzania. It is rare in India and has been seen only a few times in Sri Lanka. It lives on inland lakes and in coastal areas.

Black-crowned Night Heron (*Nycticorax nycticorax*) The night herons feed principally at dusk and near dawn, but may be active at any time during the night. During the day they roost in trees and bushes. They are found across the world wherever there are shallow marshes.

Eastern Reef Heron (*Egretta Sacra*)   Here is an example of the reef heron in its white phase. While associated with ocean reefs in its feeding, the Eastern Reef Heron is often found in tidal creeks, lagoons and mangrove swamps, never far from salt water.

Tricolored Heron (*Egretta tricolor*) Living mostly in coastal areas from New England to Peru, this bird has been reclassified in recent years from the genus *Hydranassa*, and was formerly known as the Louisiana Heron. It is uncommon throughout its range.

Purple Heron (*Ardea purpurea*) This gorgeous bird has feathers of many colors, but purple is not among them. It stands about 30 inches high, and is cautious and reclusive. It summers to central Europe and resides in swamps and reed beds in Africa, Asia and Sri Lanka.

Right: Tricolored Heron (*Egretta tricolor*) Although it does not appear so here, this heron has a very long slender neck which, with its long bill, it uses effectively to stab fish. It wades in deeper water than most other herons and stirs the bottom with its feet in order to disturb small fish.

Gray Heron (*Ardea cinerea*) This large heron, similar to the Great Blue Heron of the Americas, nests from Ireland, through Europe to Africa and Asia. It nests in colonies, usually in trees, but sometimes in reed beds, and feeds on fish in both fresh and salt water.

Eastern Reef Heron (*Egretta sacra*) The Reef Heron appears in two color phases, uniform gray with yellowish legs, as pictured here, or pure white, again with yellow legs and a yellow bill. It lives on islands and coastal shores in the area between the Indian and Pacific Oceans. The white phase is dominant in the centre of the range, the gray near the periphery.

Right: Cattle Egret (*Bubulcus ibis*) The Cattle Egret is a small white heron with a large, rounded head. In flight, it resembles the Snowy Egret, but has more rapid wing beats. It is a communal bird, as can be seen here.

Little Bittern (*Ixobrychus minutus*) This 14-inch bird is one of the smallest of the heron-like birds. It ranges from Spain in the west, through much of Africa, New Guinea and Australia. The one shown here is a female, tawny brown with a dark cap. The male is much paler below and on the flanks, and has a black back.

Snowy Egret (*Egretta thula*)   A lovely bird, it ranges from the Canadian border in summer, and nests through parts of the United States south to Argentina. It was hunted almost to extinction for its plumes until early in the twentieth century when it came under protection. Since then numbers have increased substantially, and the range has expanded.

Cattle Egret (*Bubulcus ibis*)
Cattle Egrets are very common in pastures, and follow wild hoofed animals throughout most of the warmer parts of the world, as far north as southern Europe and the Canadian border. They feed on insects which are attracted to the animals on whose backs they frequently perch.

Dwarf Bittern (*Ixobrychus sturmii*)   This little bittern spends much of its time in the forest, away from water. It lives principally in the western part of Africa, from Senegal and Sudan to South Africa.

Right: Black-headed Heron (*Ardea melanocephala*)   This large heron is quite common in East Africa. The lack of rufous colors distinguishes it from the Goliath and Purple herons which are found in the same region. It frequently feeds on grasshoppers and other insects well away from water.

Black-headed Heron
(*Ardea melanocephala*)
This black and white
heron is similar to, but
smaller and slimmer
than the Gray Heron. It
is distinguished from it
by the black head and
neck, contrasting white
chin and throat, and
gray underparts. It is
found in Africa
anywhere south of
Senegal and Ethiopia.

Reddish Egret (*Egretta rufescens*)   The bird shown here is an immature and lacks the bright rufous head and the plumes which hang like a beard down the front. The Reddish Egret is uncommon throughout its range from the extreme southern United States to Panama. When fishing it spreads its wings like a mantle, and "dances" about in the water.

Great Egret (*Casmerodius albus*) Although the Great Egret did not come as close to extirpation as the Snowy, its numbers were seriously reduced by the early twentieth century. Plumes were most valuable during the nesting season and young birds starved in the nest when the parents were shot.

Squacco Heron (*Ardeola ralloides*)   A small heron of Africa, southern Europe and southwest Asia. During the breeding season, long pale plumes grow from the back of the head, and the back becomes tawny. The wings are mostly white, but this is apparent only when the bird flies.

White-faced Heron (*Ardea novaehollandiae*) The White-faced Heron is medium-sized and lives from Australia to Indonesia in both coastal and inland environments. It feeds in shallow water and in grass, and nests in trees. In flight the primary feathers are dark with a pale bank in the middle and dark again at the leading edge.

White-backed Night Heron (*Nycticorax leuconotus*)   An unusual feature of
this heron is the prominent white eye ring. It is seen here nesting in
mangroves. It lives in West Africa southward from Senegal to Natal, Angola
and Sudan.

IBISES, SPOONBILLS, AND FLAMINGOS

Andean Flamingo (*Phoenicoparrus andinus*) Somewhat larger than the Puna Flamingo, the Andean has a rosier upper breast. It also lives in the Puna zone of Peru as well as in Chile, Bolivia and Argentina. In winter, it descends from the highland salt lakes to lowland salt marshes.

Herons, storks, ibises, spoonbills, and flamingos all belong, taxonomically, to the same order of birds — the Ciconiiformes. All feed almost entirely on animal matter, most of which is taken from the water, including such delicacies as fish, toads, snakes, salamanders, insects, worms, crustacea, and plankton. In this order of birds the ibis, spoonbill, and flamingo have some of the most interesting and colorful bills that are remarkably adapted to their manner of feeding. They also rank among the world's most spectacularly beautiful birds.

Perhaps the most memorable bird-sighting in my own experience was the fly-in of Scarlet Ibis to the Caroni Swamp near Port of Spain in Trinidad. Thousands of birds dispersed during the day to feed on mud flats and marshes throughout the area, returning towards dusk in groups of five to twenty to roost communally in the mangrove "islands" of the Caroni. Local boatmen did well taking groups on long tours of this extensive and beautiful swamp, where we saw some 50 species of marsh-loving birds during the afternoon. The climax was the ibis arrival. The boat was moored to a stake 200 yards or so from isolated patches of mature mangrove growing out of the water. Arriving in their small groups, these mixed flocks of mature and immature birds made a startling sight — the scarlet adults with their black wing-tips, long trailing legs and decurved bills, and the immatures, dusky above and white below. After flying about, the flocks settled restlessly in the green mangrove, making a sparkling picture of scarlet and white, like candles on an old-fashioned Christmas tree. When we were there immatures dominated, for many mature birds had migrated to nearby Venezuela.

There are some 25 species of ibises present on all continents, mostly in tropical and sub-tropical regions. In North America, however, the White-faced Ibis nests as far north as the Canadian border through the central United States and the Glossy Ibis is found in Maine. The White Ibis lives in coastal areas in the south and in Central and South America. The Glossy Ibis is widespread, for it has almost a world-wide distribution. The Sacred Ibis, white-bodied with a black neck, head and fluffy tail plumes, lives in Africa, west Asia and the southwest Pacific. It was revered by the early Egyptians but is no longer present in Egypt.

All of the ibises have long bills that curve downward. They and the spoonbills, which have long bills flattened laterally near the tip, find their food almost entirely by feel rather than sight. They probe in the mud or, in the case of the spoonbills, move their bill from side to side under the water, capturing their prey and working it up the bill. Food taken is similar to that of herons but includes a larger ratio of fiddler crabs and crayfish. They discard the large claw if it is too big to manage. The practice of feeding by touch, or feel, is remarkably effective for these birds. Reaction time is almost instantaneous, as stimulation of the sensitive nerves in the bill causes it to snap shut on the prey. This sensitivity enables the bird to feed in mud, among reeds, in murky water, and at night.

Nesting habits of the various ibis and spoonbill species differ considerably. The Green Ibis nests in Venezuela during the rainy season while the Buff-necked does so when it is dry. In Australia and central Africa, where rains are sporadic, nesting takes place as opportunity occurs. Rains bring dried ponds alive, rousing the animal life that may have been dormant for more than a year and providing food for probing birds. Response is quick and nesting may begin almost at once. Spoonbills and ibises in these conditions are nomadic rather than migratory, for they follow the rains. From first nesting to fledging the young takes from two to three months for most species. When the rains fail the birds do not nest.

Because flamingos live, for the most part, in remote places — soda lakes, and mud flats high in salinity — relatively few people see them in the wild. Despite this, there are few children who are not familiar with them from drawings and from seeing their plastic replicas on suburban lawns. Their unusual shape and predominant pinkness is both unmistakable and unforgettable.

Over the years of scientific disagreement, flamingos of the family Phoenicopteridae have been allied with several different groups of birds. There appears, even today, to be some dissension concerning the common names of the five (or six) species and their classification into species and subspecies. It is enough to be aware that the bright pink flamingos seen in the Caribbean are Phoenicoperus ruber and known to some as the Caribbean Flamingo, and that those in southern Europe and North Africa, there known as Greater Flamingos, are of the same species, but are much paler. Other species are the James, or Puna Flamingo, which lives to about 13,000 feet in saline lakes in the Andes, and the Andean Flamingo, which lives at lower altitudes.

The bodies and necks of most species are white, with much pink on the wings, which also have black flight feathers. The long legs and turned-downed bill are pink in adults and black among the young.

All flamingos feed on algae, diatoms, and invertebrates, some concentrating more on brine flies which they strain through their bill.

They invert the bill when feeding so that it is held upside down. The tongue acts as a piston, which forces the mud and water through filters known as lamellae.

When the monogamous pairs nest they scoop mud into a pile, as high as 12 inches, on which the female usually lays only one egg. Incubation, which is shared, takes about a month, after which the down-covered chick takes a further 75 days until fledged. Flamingos, in common only with pigeons, feed the young on a secretion, rich in protein and fat, which is generated in the crop. Chicks emerge with straight bills and are incapable of feeding themselves until the bill grows the great hook. Thus, the parents of most species continue feeding the young their "milk" until they are fledged. As they grow, young birds are a dingy brown, gradually emerging with the pink and white of mature birds, a process that takes three or four years. They do not usually breed until they are fully mature.

Flamingos nest in great colonies throughout their disjunctive range, which extends from South America in the west to India in the east. The colonies usually contain thousands of birds, but the isolated and small group in the Galapagos have as few as three to five pairs. Flamingos are threatened everywhere by climate, disaster, poachers, and zoo collectors. Since their feathers fade, they were not popular as millinery items when ladies wore plumes. The colony in the Bahamas was much disturbed by local people hunting for food. They would stretch wires along the mud upwind of nesting birds, and drive them towards the wire, which was pulled taut as the birds approached. The mangled birds were then collected. The colony in the Camargue in the south of France is reasonably protected, as is the group on the mud flats at the entrance to the harbor at Tunis.

Flamingos are long-lived birds, although the average life span is considerably shorter than the 50 or even 60 years that some are known to have survived in the wild. Thus, although each pair may produce only one egg per year, by the time of death the pair may have raised a considerable number of young. Many colonies under protection remain relatively stable and should continue this way as long as their habitat is not unduly affected.

White Ibis (*Eudocimus albus*) This handsome ibis nests in coastal swamps and mangroves from the southern United States to Peru. The scarlet legs indicate that the bird is nesting. It is gregarious, flying about in flocks in search of food.

Roseate Spoonbill (*Ajaia ajaja*)   Spoonbills feed by swinging their heads
from side to side in shallow water, straining their food out from the mud on
the lake bottom. This is the only western hemisphere spoonbill. It lives from
Florida, through the West Indies to northern Argentina. It nests in rookeries,
which it shares with herons and ibises.

Scarlet Ibis (*Eudocimus ruber*)   This wonderful bird lives in northern South America and Trinidad and, occasionally, is seen in Jamaica, Grenada and Tobago. The adult, pictured here, is in full color. It nests in colonies in trees or mangroves, and feeds by probing in the mud for small crustaceans. It also takes fish and insects.

African Spoonbill (*Platalae alba*) Its red face and legs distinguish this spoonbill from the European Spoonbill. The spatula-like bill is typical of each of the world's six spoonbill species. This one is found in shallow lakes and marshes from Ethiopia to Zimbabwe.

Right: Royal Spoonbill (*Platalae regia*) The tufts hanging from the neck indicate that this bird is in breeding plumage. The habitat shown here is not typical, however, for it generally feeds in shallow water. The Royal Spoonbill is resident in Indonesia, New Guinea and Australia. It has recently extended its range to New Zealand.

Australian White Ibis (*Threskiornis moluccus*) The decurved bill, in this case quite long, is typical of the ibis group. This one lives in the northeastern part of Australia, particularly near the coast, but it moves inland during the rains. It also ranges to New Guinea and Indonesia. The head and neck of mature birds are unfeathered.

Greater Flamingo (*Phoenicopterus ruber*)   This species is widely distributed in northern South America, the Caribbean, Europe, Asia, and Africa. The Caribbean race, pictured here, is quite vivid. The eastern races in Europe and Africa are pale, almost white, with the exception of the leading edge of the wing which is bright red. The flight feathers are black.

James or Puna Flamingo (*Phoenicoparrus jamesi*)   This small flamingo is best known as a resident of Lake Titicaca high in the Peruvian Andes, although it also appears in the highlands of Bolivia and northwestern Argentina. This is the smallest of the three flamingo species in the Andes.

Puna Ibis (*Plegadis ridgwayi*)   This dark ibis stands 22 inches high. It lives in the Puna zone of the Andes at 12,000 to 13,000 feet, frequenting swamps and ponds. The range extends from Peru to Bolivia, but it is seen occasionally in northern Argentina.

Left: Greater Flamingo (*Phoenicopterus ruber*)   The distinctive curved bill on flamingos develops only after the immature stage of growth. During early life, when it is being fed, the bill is straight. It is capable of feeding itself only when the bill can be inverted for straining the algae which is its food.

Glossy Ibis (*Plegadis falcinellus*)   This lovely bird, which appears to be black in flight, is distributed through most parts of the world. In Europe it does not appear west of northern Italy. In North America the range is being extended northward, and it now nests to Maine. Unlike most marsh birds the Glossy Ibis often flies in lines.

Lesser Flamingo (*Phoeniconsias minor*)   This flamingo stands about 40 inches tall, compared to the 56 inches of the Greater. The bill is much redder, and the feathers have a darker hue. The two million birds present on Lake Natron in Tanzania have been much photographed. The range extends to India and Madagascar.

Sacred Ibis (*Threskiornis aethiopica*)   Young birds are feathered on the head and neck, but at maturity these areas are black and naked. The Sacred Ibis is fairly common on tidal flats, in marshes, pastures and swamps in East Africa, western Asia and in the southwest Pacific.

Straw-necked Ibis (*Threskiornis spinicollis*)   This Australian bird is
recognized in that country as its most valuable destroyer of harmful insects.
It feeds principally in open fields and nests in bushes and trees. It is
common in many parts of Australia, and wanders to New Guinea and
Tasmania.

CRANES AND LIMPKIN

Blue Crane (*Anthropoides paradisea*)   This is a non-migratory species that lives in fairly large groups in South Africa. The uniform pale gray is attractive, as is the unusually-shaped head. In appearance this bird is more like a goose than a crane.

Cranes, of which there are 15 species, together with the Limpkin, one species, are members of the order known as Gruiformes, which also includes the rails, sunbitterns, seriemas, and bustards. The cranes are among the most ancient families of birds, known from fossils to have existed for at least 60 million years. They are remarkable in several ways: among them is the tallest of flying birds, standing over six feet in height, and also the loudest, whose ringing cries may be heard for a mile or more. Several of their species are seriously endangered, the Whooping Crane having been brought to the brink of extinction, aided in part by a hurricane in 1940. Of the others the Siberian, the Red-crowned, and the Black-necked each have populations of under 1,000 birds. The story of the survival and rehabilitation of the Whooping Crane is well known. This giant bird once bred in wetlands over much of central North America. During the nineteenth century it was heavily shot for food in the prairies, and progressive drainage for agriculture reduced its nesting area and habitat in the region now known as Wood Buffalo National Park in Alberta and the Northwest Territories. This nesting area remained undiscovered for many years, but a few birds migrated each year to the Aransas National Wildlife Refuge in Texas. By 1941 there were only two wintering areas still in use, Aransas and another in Louisiana where a hurricane killed every bird. That left 11 birds in Aransas. The story of the recovery effort is too long to tell here, except to say that some crippled birds were taken into captivity and a program was undertaken to lift one egg, of two, from nests in the far north and place them under wild female Sandhill Cranes. These carefully planned programs have been quite successful. Whooping Cranes now fly with the Sandhills from the central prairies to a more southerly wintering area, thus dispersing the remaining whoopers, but these displaced birds have not yet nested. The Whooping Crane has been saved from extinction by man, who put it in peril, but its hold is tenuous. These giant birds require a thousand acres or more per pair for nesting and maintain large territories in winter. Aransas is as full as it can reasonably be and it is not at all safe. Across the marshes one can see oil rigs in the Gulf of Mexico, and large barges filled with oil and chemicals pass by the edge of the marsh in full view of feeding birds.

Cranes are found all around the world — from the Arctic to southern Australia. The more numerous species have adjusted to and benefitted from man's activities during the past few thousand years. They now feed on seeds and grasses in agricultural areas and aid farmers by eating harmful insects. Some crane species feed entirely in marshes and at the margins of ponds, but all nest in damp areas, building platforms. During the period before the eggs are laid, mated birds emit loud cries to one another, advertising their territory which they defend vigorously. Most species lay two eggs, but it is seldom that more than one chick survives to fledge. In the case of the Whooping Crane this permits the removal of one egg before hatching. Young birds learn their feeding habits from the parents and migrate with them, remaining attached until the next breeding season when they are driven away. Chicks are feathered upon emerging from the egg and soon follow their parents about the marsh.

Cranes range in height from three to nearly seven feet, and weigh from six to twenty-three pounds. They have white or gray bodies, dark wingtips, and long slender legs. The neck and facial markings vary considerably, some being very beautiful. When they fly the neck is held straight in front, unlike herons which generally fly with the neck curved back. The long legs and relatively small feet trail behind.

The Limpkin, the only member of the family Aramidae, is similar in structure to the cranes, but its digestive functions have more in common with those of rails. It is a rather nondescript brown bird covered with white flecks, and having a long, slightly down-curved bill and long legs. It stands about two and a half feet tall. When walking at the edge of the fresh water marsh the Limpkin has an unusual rolling gait that makes it appear to be limping — from this stems its name. Although its feet are unwebbed it is a good swimmer.

The principal and indispensable item of the Limpkin's diet is a species of freshwater snail that is normally found on the mud or under the surface. The snail is snapped up and carried to the shore, where it is quickly opened and consumed. The presence of Limpkins can usually be established by large numbers of empty shells lining the shore of a pond. It also feeds on frogs and worms, but must have snails to survive. Draining of marshes has reduced the Limpkin's range in the United States to southern Florida, but it is present in modest numbers throughout suitable areas of Central and South America. It appears as a solitary bird for the most part.

Crowned Crane (*Balearica pavonina*) In the wild this crane is found in West Africa, from Senegal south to Nigeria. Its spectacular yellowish crown and blocks of color — blue, straw, white and maroon — as well as its great height, make it a glamor bird in captivity.

Limpkin (*Aramus guarauna*)   This rather awkward and ordinary-looking
marsh bird has the distinction of being the only member of its family. It
lives in fresh water marshes and swamps, from the southern United States
to Argentina, searching for the snails which it must have to survive. It
opens the snails at the edge of the water, leaving the shells in a pile.

Left: Damoiselle Crane (*Anthropoides virgo*)   This dainty crane nests in eastern Europe, North Africa and in Asia east to Mongolia. It winters in India, Pakistan and Burma where it feeds, not only on insects and reptiles, but on green shoots of emerging grain. It is a target for eager guns. The roar of large flocks on takeoff can be heard for miles.

Sandhill Crane (*Grus canadensis*)   This western hemisphere species nests to the high Arctic and in marshes across the central plains of Canada and the United States. It migrates in flocks to winter in the southern United States and Mexico, often flying so high that it cannot be seen from the ground.

Whooping Crane (*Grus americana*)   The fifty-year battle to save the Whooping Crane from extinction is well known. In 1940 only 11 birds survived a devastating hurricane. Wild birds now nest in Wood Buffalo Park in northern Canada and winter principally in the Aransas Refuge in southern Texas. The migration journey between these areas is full of perils.

Right: Red-crowned Crane (*Grus japonensis*)   Of the world's 15 species of cranes six are endangered. There are only about 1,000 Red-crowned Cranes remaining in the wild. The tail, which is not shown here, stands out from the rear like a great feather duster. It lives in Japan, Korea, and China.

Australian or Brolga Crane (*Grus rubicunda*)   The Brolga Crane is similar to the more widely distributed and better-known Sarus Crane, and is a uniform gray with red facial markings. It lives in New Guinea and throughout much of northern and eastern Australia. It feeds in marshes and meadows and nests on the ground beside suitable ponds.

RAILS

Water Rail (*Rallus aquaticus*)   This is a hardy northern bird of the eastern hemisphere. It is present throughout the year in most of Europe and Asia, withdrawing in winter only from areas which freeze. Seldom seen in summer, it remains deep in the reeds, but its various grunts and clucks confirm its presence. In rough weather it moves more readily into the open.

The 124 or so species of rails are present all over the world, except at the northern and southern extremes. They live in a variety of habitats — some walk about in the dense reeds of the marshes, some swim while taking their food, and some forage in field and forest. Those that feed mostly on dry land are seldom far from water. Most rail species are reclusive, living in rank marshes, and they are one of the least-studied families of birds. Some species are known to lay as many as 16 eggs in a clutch of which perhaps half survive to fledge. The parents with large broods appear to favor a few chicks for feeding, leaving the others to fend for themselves and sometimes to starve. In some species nesting takes place in a group, with females copulating with a number of males and several females laying in the same nest. In this case communal care and feeding of the young is common.

For convenience, rails may be divided into three groups which, while having some overlap, have different characteristics. The first group consists of short-billed rails, the bills not being long enough to probe effectively in the mud for worms and grubs. These rails take their food, mostly invertebrate, while exploring their marsh or dry land habitat. They are slim, narrow birds adapted to moving about in the dense vegetation that is their home. It is this characteristic that gives us the expression "thin as a rail." Some species in this group live almost entirely on vegetable matter. This gives them more flexibility in feeding than those species that rely on animal matter living in soft mud for their food. The short-billed group, including the gallinules and crakes, has the largest number of species. The gallinules are less reclusive than some species for they feed extensively at the water margin and on lily pads. The beautifully-colored Purple Gallinule, which lives from the southern United States to Argentina, may be easily seen in Florida and in marshes across the south. The similarly-named European Purple Gallinule, or Purple Swamphen, lives from southern Europe to Australia. The Common Moorhen is widely distributed throughout the world. Gallinules and moorhens swim readily but don't spend as much time in the water as in the marsh. All have rather stout legs and four enormously long toes, one of which is at the back of the leg. The Corncrake, which lives south from northern Asia to Africa, is a drab ten-inch bird with chestnut-colored wings, and has legs that dangle when it flies. It is shy and seldom seen, feeding in grasslands and hayfields, but its rasping *crex, crex* cry makes it easy to locate. The Corncrake was once common all over Europe, but intensive farming methods and the heavy use of pesticides have narrowed its range to remote areas. It has now disappeared from England, occurs only on migration to Ireland and Scotland, and is rare in southern Europe.

The rails of the second group have medium to long bills, which they use to probe for worms, and for crushing insects. Most members of this group live deep in the marsh and are seen only when they venture from it. Their strange chatter — an odd mixture of grunts, clucks, and squawks — tells us where they are. Among this group is the Water Rail, widespread in Europe and Asia, and similar in pattern and size to the Virginia Rail, which lives from Canada to Peru. The other North American species with long bills are the 15-inch King and Clapper Rails, the latter living only in salt marshes near the coast. Little is known of the social habits of long-billed rails. They appear in a suitable area for a year or two, and after that move on. They are known to be fiercely territorial. The wood-rails of Central and South America are attractive birds that walk about in the dense undergrowth of the forest, taking their food from the forest floor.

The third group consists of some ten species of coots. These are aquatic birds and the best known of the rails, for they swim readily into open water and often congregate in rafts of thousands of birds in winter. It is among the coots that we find the most elaborate and extensive frontal shields, fleshy and colorful extensions of the upper mandible, which may stretch across the forehead to behind the eyes. This shield grows at the beginning of the nesting season and may well play a part in mate selection and in territorial protection. The Horned Coot, which lives on lakes high in the Andes, has a frilled extension of the upper mandible that stretches from its tip to behind the eyes.

When swimming, coots poke their heads forward with each stroke of the lobed feet. For much of the year coots feed on vegetable matter, most of which they gather while diving to the bottom. They must return to the surface to eat and one sees them with trailing masses of green stuff hanging from their bills. More assertive individuals do not trouble to dive but feed by stealing the weeds gathered by others. During the nesting season the diet contains a predominance of insects. Coots, which do not seek the protection of vegetation, have developed more robust and wider bodies than the short-billed rails.

Coots in Europe were once heavily shot for sport and food in winter. One reads of royal shoots on the Norfolk Broads when it was not unheard of to kill 1,000 birds in a day. One participant was King George V, who recorded many such shoots in his game diary. Puntguns, fearsome weapons mounted as cannons and charged with a pound of powder, might account for 50 or more birds with a single blast.

Several rail species have become extinct during the last hundred years, some by persecution and some through loss of habitat. Many species have emerged as a result of evolution in isolation on a single remote island. Some of these are now endangered, for populations of all animals without a wide distribution are exposed to many perils besides man.

European or Common Coot (*Fulica atra*) The European Coot has a large white frontal shield which is missing in the American Coot. It is widespread and common from the United Kingdom to Australia. In flight it shows a white wing bar. Generally found in ponds and marshes, it has taken to city parks in large numbers.

American Purple Gallinule (*Porphyrula martinica*) This species has a yellow-tipped red bill and a sky blue frontal shield. It nests from the southern United States to Argentina, but some numbers wander much farther north. The shades of blue on the forepart of this bird shimmer in the sunlight.

Purple Swamphen (*Porphyrio porphyrio*)   This eastern hemisphere species has a large red frontal shield. It is widely distributed in fresh water marshes and swamps from southern Spain, through Asia to Australia. The long toes are not lobed.

Clapper Rail (*Rallus longirostris*)
The Clapper is found in salt
marshes around the southern and
eastern United States and in South
America to Peru and Brazil. It
occasionally hybridizes with King
Rails in areas where their ranges
overlap. It may be heard as it gives
its fast and then slow *kek, kek, kek*
call.

Red-knobbed or Crested Coot
(*Fulica cristata*)   This large coot is
both resident and migrant from
Ethiopia to South Africa, with a
separate population in southern
Spain, Portugal and Morocco. It
has two red knobs on top of the
large white frontal shield, a
characteristic which is only
distinguishable at short range.

Sora (*Porzana carolina*) Some rails, including the Sora, are common in both brackish and fresh water marshes, but are difficult to spot. They can be found by their *ker-wee* calls, and may be tempted to the edge of the thick marsh plants by playing the call on a tape. They nest throughout most of North America and south as far as Peru.

Weka (*Gallirallus australis*)   About the size of a chicken, the Weka of New Zealand is a flightless rail with strong feet and reduced wings. Its plumage is usually brown and black.

Right: Virginia Rail (*Rallus limicola*)   Three western hemisphere rails are similar in appearance — the King, Clapper, and Virginia. Of these the last is the smallest at about 10 inches. All have long, slightly down-curved bills.

Left: Common Moorhen (*Gallinula chloropus*) The Moorhen and the Coot are the two rails that habitually swim while foraging. They swim to the bottom of a pond or marsh and bring growing plants to the surface. This species has worldwide distribution, nesting in North America to southern Canada and in Europe to Scandinavia.

American Coot (*Fulica americana*) The American Coot is an abundant species, nesting in fresh water marshes from northern Canada to Argentina. It winters as far north as it can find open water, both fresh and salt. The ones pictured here appear to have been left behind by winter. The toes of coots are lobed to assist them in their swimming.

White-spotted Pygmy Crake (*Sarothrura pulchra*)   This tiny crake appears from West Africa eastward to Uganda and Kenya. It lives deep in swampy forests, and although it is seldom seen, one can often hear its bell-like note.

JACANAS

Lotus Bird (*Jacana gallinacea*) Jacanas have long legs with very long spindly toes and straight nails. This enables them to walk about on the floating vegetation where they feed and nest. This is the only Australian jacana which lives in the north and down the east coast. The adult is distinguished by the brilliant red comb on its forehead.

The jacanas are often known as lily-trotters because of their habit of running about on lily pads and lotus leaves. They are about nine to twelve inches long but are able, because of extremely long slender toes and almost straight claws, to be supported on floating vegetation. They live on ponds and slow-flowing rivers in tropical Central and South America, as well as Africa, Southeast Asia, and Northern Australia.

Jacanas form a small family of birds — seven or eight species, depending on which authority is used. Some consider the Northern (or American) and Wattled Jacanas of the Western Hemisphere to be conspecific, while others consider them to be separate, despite the hybridization that is known to occur. All are strongly-marked, attractive birds, some with flashy patterns. Five of the species have fleshy shields above the bill, sometimes extending behind the eyes, in a range of bright colors that includes red, yellow, pale gray, and bright blue. They feed on a mixture of seeds from water plants, insects, mollusks, and the occasional small fish.

Nesting takes place during wet periods when ponds and rivers are full and when insect-hatching is at its peak. In most species nest building, incubation, and care of the young is carried out by the male alone. In areas where water is patchy, one female may mate with several males during the same nesting period, laying a clutch in successive nests. Eggs are often laid and incubated on a large floating leaf, but usually a simple nest will be made in matted vegetation. While females do not participate in nesting or care of the young, they do share in defending the territory. Along the banks of rivers, where there is more nesting space, jacanas appear to be monogamous, each pair defending its own stretch of river.

All species have long thin legs that propel their remarkable feet, and all but the Pheasant-tailed Jacana have short tails. This beautiful bird has a down-curving tail that is almost as long as its body. When I first saw this bird on a pond in Sri Lanka I was not familiar with it, and wondered what kind of pheasant could be sitting on the water. The Pheasant-tailed Jacana incubates the eggs, two under each wing, away from the edge of the pond. Its black body and tail, white flanks and face, and bright yellow nape are quite startling.

Jacanas are capable of swimming, although they do not do so under normal conditions. The African Jacana is known to submerge when alarmed, with only the bill and nostrils remaining above the surface. Usually jacanas live in flat country at low elevations, but in India some are known to nest as high as 5,000 feet. During the non-breeding season they become nomadic and, following water, congregate in groups of up to 100 birds. In some villages jacanas become quite tame, disregarding the people who use the water.

African Jacana (*Actophilornis africana*) The bright chestnut plumage
identifies this jacana, which is widely distributed in Central and East Africa
where permanent water permits the growth of lilies and other aquatic
vegetation.

PLOVERS AND OYSTERCATCHERS

Killdeer (*Charadrius vociferus*)   The Killdeer is the best-known plover in North America, for it nests in fields and at the edge of suburban lawns. Its loud *kill-dee* call echoes whenever it flies.

Much confusion has existed among taxonomists regarding the classification of several species of plovers and sandpipers; one or two species now recognized as sandpipers are still known as plovers in their common names. Many members of both families feed together on shores and mud flats during migration, and seem to be the same birds to the casual observer. Typically, plovers are similar to sandpipers in that they are pale or white on the underparts and brown above. Also, plovers have shorter, thicker bills, with a swelling at the tip, rather like pigeons. Most species that feed on the shore have one or several rings across the throat and a black forehead.

Among the 62 to 70 species of the plover family are a dozen known as lapwings and half a dozen known as dotterels. Most plovers, like sandpipers, have pointed wings and are fast, strong fliers. The lapwings, however, have broader, rounded wings and are noted for their aerial displays, usually close to a nest site and near the ground. Plovers range in size from 6 to 16 inches, and live in every part of the world that is not permanently frozen. Some are dry land birds but most live near the water.

The northern nesting species of plovers are strongly migratory, often undertaking extraordinarily long non-stop flights over water. Some flocks of the Lesser (or American) Golden Plover, which nest in the high Arctic of North America, drift eastward to Labrador and Newfoundland where they feed voraciously for a week or so on berries, in order to build fat. They then undertake a direct flight of approximately 2,500 miles to the shores of Guiana or Brazil. They are capable of resting briefly on the ocean, but autumn storms cause many exhausted birds to drown. Other flocks of Lesser Golden Plovers make the long non-stop journey from Alaska to Hawaii — some 2,800 miles in 50 or more hours. Black-bellied Plovers tend to follow coastlines or migrate inland, resting on the way. Some of these birds winter in the southern United States, but others continue on as far as Chile. Plovers breeding in northern Asia migrate to winter as far south as Australia, and several species that live permanently in temperate or tropical areas do not migrate at all.

Most sandpipers wade while feeding, picking their food from the surface or from the bottom. Plovers, on the other hand, run about on the soft mud of water margins, or in damp areas nearby. Black-bellied and Golden Plovers migrate in flocks and are often seen feeding in stubble or in pastures. They capture insects, mollusks, beetles, and worms, and eat berries on occasion.

All migratory birds face a host of perils, both natural and artificial, on their twice-yearly journeys. Most perching birds find suitable feeding and resting places along the way. Shorebirds are reliant on marshes and mud flats on either salt or fresh water. They migrate in large flocks and must find extensive areas where they may stay for several days, in order to regain body fat for the next leg of the journey. In North America, particularly on the eastern seaboard, such resting places are disappearing. Urban sprawl has brought houses and multiple dwellings to the edge of the beaches; marshes are being drained for development of all kinds; and vehicles charge up and down the beaches. All of this puts pressure on resting birds, which become harried and stressed. Southbound plovers and sandpipers start appearing as early as July, having left the young birds of the season to follow when they are fully fledged and strong. This is the peak time for human use of beaches. Those birds that migrate inland are better off, for fresh water marshes tend to be more remote. It is likely that the reduction of protected beaches has led to decline in shorebird populations.

During the present century the nature of pressure on shorebirds has changed. During the nineteenth century and earlier, vast numbers of migrating shorebirds were shot for food, and a great number for sport. The Migratory Birds Act of 1918 protected all species of North American shorebirds (except the snipe and woodcock, which are still shot), but not until the populations of some species had been drastically reduced. The Golden Plover was heading for extinction, following the Eskimo Curlew, a sandpiper that may now be gone. Market gunners filled their wagons, the tiny birds selling in Boston and New York at ten cents a dozen. By this time there were no more Passenger Pigeons to shoot for they were gone as a product for market by the 1880s.

Those species that rely on beaches in populated areas as breeding grounds are in serious trouble. The little Piping Plover, which nests on the eastern seaboard of North America and in the central plains, has disappeared from most of its coastal range. Its nest, a simple scrape on the beach not far above the tide line, is extremely vulnerable unless the beach is closed to humans and animals. One of the few remote places left is in the Magdalen Islands in the Gulf of St. Lawrence, where the eggs are laid on the windswept beaches and subject to washouts during the frequent storms. Even there, only 35 pairs were found in 1990.

The most widely distributed and best-known plover in North America is the Killdeer, a bird that does not require a wet habitat. It nests almost anywhere on farms and in suburban areas, even sometimes under the wheels of cars in driveways. It is noisy, even when undisturbed, flying about shouting *"killdee, killdee."* It is this bird that almost everyone has seen doing its broken-wing act, feigning injury while leading an intruder from eggs or young.

Most plovers lay four eggs, although the range is two to six. The young hatch alert and feathered, capable of moving about within hours. They instinctively start pecking at tiny insects. The Arctic nesters must grow quickly to prepare themselves to fly south by August.

The Oystercatchers live only in coastal areas throughout the world, as far north as Scandinavia and as far south as South Africa and Australia. There are between 6 and 11 species, depending upon which authority is used, and as many as 21 subspecies. All have long, heavy, red bills of considerable strength. They are among the largest of shorebirds, having a length of 15 to 18 inches and weighing up to 27 ounces. As a family they are relatively uniform in size and pattern. Some are pure black while others show various patterns of black and white. They have relatively heavy legs.

Oystercatchers feed, when possible, almost exclusively on mollusks, either bivalves such as clams, oysters, and mussels, or on snails that they take on the surface or by digging in the mud. If they find a bivalve with its shell open they drive their bills into the gap and dislocate the muscle holding the two shells together. If the mollusk is closed the shell is bashed open with the bird's bill. Young birds are unable to feed themselves in this manner for some time and rely on the parents. They soon learn to find easier food to deal with than mollusks and become partially independent.

Unlike most other shorebirds, oystercatchers breed only when they are three to five years old. During breeding season the adolescents group in attendant flocks, while nesting birds maintain defended territories. Displays by nesting birds are frequent, and include posturing with the neck arched and the bill almost touching the ground, while calling with a piping note. The two or three eggs are laid in sand or among pebbles, and require nearly a month of incubation. Young birds fledge at about 30 days. Because of the exposed positions in which they lay clutches, they are subject to heavy predation. It is not unusual for a pair to lay three or more clutches in one season before the eggs survive to hatch.

Crowned Lapwing or Plover (*Stephanibyx coronatus*) Its distinct and handsome markings make this an unusually elegant bird. It lives in inland country from East and Central Africa to South Africa in bush, grassy plains, and sometimes in cultivated areas.

Kittlitz's Sandplover (*Charadrius pecuarius*)   This small African plover is
quite dark on the back, with buff-colored underparts. It lives on coastal or
inland mud and sand flats in central and eastern Africa. It is not afraid of
humans, and often feeds in flocks in grassy areas near water.

Snowy Plover (*Charadrius alexandrinus*)   A pale little plover which nests on sandy beaches in Europe, Africa and North America. It has a neck ring during the nesting season, usually incomplete in females. The population is small and is declining, principally because of disturbance on its nesting beaches.

Left: Masked Plover (*Vanellus miles*) The Masked Plover nests only in northern Australia and southern New Guinea, but is seen in most of the eastern part of Australia. It feeds on grasslands and mud flats, but is most evident in suburban areas where it frequents lawns. The large yellow wattles are the distinguishing feature.

Wilson's Plover (*Charadrius wilsonia*) The bird shown here is a female at the nest. It breeds occasionally along the eastern seaboard of the United States, and south to Panama and northeastern Brazil. It nests on sandy beaches well above the tide line, scraping a hollow and lining it with bits of wood. The male has a heavy black line across the breast.

European Oystercatcher (*Haematopus ostralegus*)   A hardy bird, it is a year-round resident in southern Iceland and Sweden, Britain, and along the Atlantic coast of Europe. It nests in Arctic Europe and Asia, and as far south as Australia. Some move inland to feed in fields and river banks.

Semi-palmated Plover (*Charadrius semipalmatus*) Named because of the partial webbing between the toes, this seven-inch bird nests in the Canadian Arctic and Alaska, and migrates in huge numbers to winter from the southern coasts of the United States to southern Argentina.

Black-bellied Plover (*Pluvialis squatarola*) Nesting all around the high Arctic, the Black-bellied Plover migrates through North America and Europe. Some winter around the shores of North America, some in Europe and the United Kingdom. Others go as far as Australia, South Africa and southern South America.

Chestnut-banded Sandplover (*Charadrius venustus*)   This handsome plover is found only on the soda lakes of East Africa, Lake Magadi in southern Kenya and Lakes Manyara and Natron in Tanzania. The chestnut-colored band distinguishes it from the Ringed Plover, which has a broad black band.

Right: Three-banded Plover (*Charadrius tricollaris*)   Despite its name, this African species has only two dark bands across the chest. Although it is an inland species which frequents the shores of lakes, rivers and ponds, it does, on occasion, visit coastal lagoons.

American Oystercatcher (*Haematopus palliatus*)   As we see in this photograph, oystercatchers nest in hard surroundings. When the young emerge from the egg they are active almost immediately. This species nests along the coast of the United States north to New Jersey.

Ringed Plover (*Charadrius hiaticula*)   This is probably the most numerous of the shorebirds in Europe and Asia. It nests in the far north and around the Baltic and the United Kingdom, where it remains in winter. Many birds migrate to central and eastern Africa. It nests on sandy and pebbled shores and winters on mud flats.

Ruddy Turnstone (*Arenaria interpres*) The colorful turnstone shown here is in full breeding plumage. In winter it loses the chestnut mantle. Turnstones are circumpolar in breeding distribution, nesting only in the far north of North America and Europe. They find their food by turning pebbles over with their bills, and snapping up sand fleas and other animal matter beneath.

Right: Black Oystercatcher (*Haematopus bachmani*) This chunky black bird with a brilliant red bill and red eyes resides from the Aleutians to Baja, California. It is a gregarious bird, flocking along rocky shores at all times of the year, and feeding on mussels, clams and oysters. Its strong bill is used to open bivalves.

98

Lesser Golden Plover (*Pluvialis dominica*)   This photograph shows a bird in full breeding plumage. It nests in the Arctic of Asia and North America, and winters mostly in the southern hemisphere. North American birds migrate over the ocean in the autumn, and across the plains in spring. They are seldom seen in western Europe.

Blacksmith Plover (*Hoplopterus armatus*)   This clearly marked pied bird has a wide distribution in Africa, from the Rift Valley in southern Kenya to South Africa. It prefers a habitat near fresh or brackish water, but is seen in wooded areas at the edge of the Serengeti Plain. The name comes from its voice which resembles the sound of pieces of metal being banged together.

White-fronted Sandplover (*Charadrius marginatus*)   This rather drab plover
nests and lives on sandy coasts of East Africa and on banks of the larger
lakes of central Africa. Although it is non-migratory it moves about as
climate and local conditions demand.

SANDPIPERS, AVOCETS, AND STILTS

Pied Avocet (*Recurvirostra avosetta*)   This avocet nests in southern Europe, across Central Asia and in Africa. It prefers brackish water, soda lakes, and salt water where it swims to feed, upending like a duck.

The sandpipers, avocets, and stilts are placed together here because they tend to have longish to very long thin bills, while the plovers have stouter and shorter bills. The sandpipers, of which there are 76 to 81 species, are of the family Scolopacidae; the avocets and stilts both belong to the family Recurvirostridae, with only seven species in all. All, including the plovers, phalaropes, stone curlews, pratincoles, sheathbills, skuas, gulls, terns, skimmers, auks, murres, and puffins belong to the same order of birds, the Charadiiformes.

The sandpiper family not only includes birds known as sandpipers, but also those known as curlews, snipes, dunlins, dowitchers, yellow-legs, whimbrels, ruffs, and the willet. All have long wings in relation to the size of their bodies, short tails, and most have relatively long legs and necks. In all cases the bill is at least as long as the head, but usually quite a bit longer, and may be straight or curved. The many sandpiper species range in size from 5 to 26 inches and in weight from about half an ounce to 37 ounces.

Most people see sandpipers on coastal or inland mud flats during the spring and fall migrations. Here they congregate in large numbers, running about and either picking food from the surface or probing for it in the mud. Some species are seldom seen. Breeding woodcocks, for instance, nest in damp bush and are seen and heard mainly in their wonderful nuptial flights, climbing to great heights in the twilight and then zooming earthward with a chittering song. When settled, the male utters a *peent* sound. Other species nest and feed in grassland quite far from water, and some nest high in the mountains. In North America the Spotted Sandpiper nests from the far north to New Mexico and Texas, usually along the banks of streams and ponds where it may be seen in spring and summer teetering along, constantly bobbing its tail and flying short distances with a fast fluttering wingbeat.

Most species are strongly migratory, arriving on their northern breeding grounds around the world, often before the tundra is clear of ice. They must then subsist on berries until the fly hatch begins. They either arrive paired, or find mates within a few days in order to begin nesting without delay, for the season is short. The female usually lays four eggs and incubation begins when the last egg is laid. Most nest on the ground, lining the simple nest with grasses, the nest usually being well hidden under last year's grass or under a bush. Some individual sandpipers use old nests of songbirds. Incubation, which among most species is shared, lasts from 18 to 30 days depending principally on the size of the bird. The young run about after they hatch. For some larger species that nest in temperate areas, fledging may take as long as 50 days. Migration to winter quarters begins by early July and by the end of the month large numbers of birds are present on beaches and flats in temperate latitudes. The winter range of most species is extensive. Some North American breeders may winter as far north as New Jersey or proceed to southern South America.

Sandpipers are generally fairly uniform in shape and pattern — brown- or gray-striped and spotted above during the nesting season, and pale below. The smaller species are usually difficult to identify, for they are so small that the characteristics of the various species can only be distinguished at close range. Some have pale legs, some dark and some green. When they fly, the observer is helped by wingspan and tail pattern, which must be memorized since the view is usually fleeting. The spring patterns are more distinct than those of the autumn, by which time the birds have molted.

Like the plovers and other birds that use the shores for feeding and nesting, sandpipers lose more and more suitable habitats each year, both in Europe and North America. The far northern nesters have stable conditions for breeding, but on migration they are harried by small boys, dogs, vehicles, and pollution. Until fairly recently sandpipers, particularly the larger species like the yellowlegs, were shot in the thousands on both their spring and fall migrations. The Solitary Sandpiper, now an uncommon bird, has never recovered its numbers after being shipped by the barrel-load to market. A recovery effort has started for the Eskimo Curlew, a bird that has been seen rarely in recent years.

Plovers and sandpipers are often and aptly called the "windbirds." They evoke a sense of mystery as they appear briefly in the spring, to return some two months later after having raised their brood. They are in danger at all stages of their lives. Their only defense is the fact that they can react swiftly and effectively. An apparently peaceful flock feeding in the mud will suddenly take off in a tight group, sometimes for no apparent reason, but often because the birds have seen a predator. One September day I was watching such a group from the dunes on Prince Edward Island as a Merlin, a small falcon that feeds almost entirely on birds, stooped. It singled out a Semipalmated Sandpiper and chased it for 15 minutes, diving and turning in tight circles. The Sandpiper was able to maintain a lead for a few yards but the Merlin's swifter flight always led to its gaining. At the last moment the sandpiper would turn sharply under the Merlin and veer off in another direction. In this case the sandpiper won, for it could turn much more quickly and after a time the falcon flew off unsatisfied.

There are nine species of avocets and stilts, and several subspecies, all living in temperate and tropical habitats on both sides of the equator. They have long to very long slender legs and thin pointed bills, straight in most stilts and gracefully curved upward among the avocets.

When they fly, the contrasting black wings and pale bodies flash dramatically and the long legs trail behind. Sizes range from 12 to 20 inches, making them fairly large shorebirds. The feet are either fully or partially webbed and all are good swimmers, taking much of their food while doing so. Stilts have red legs, avocets blue-gray, and all have dark bills except the Ibisbill of the Himalayas, which has a red one. Most are lowland species living in both fresh and salt-water marshes. The Ibisbill, however, nests between 5,000 and 14,000 feet in Asia, and the Andean Avocets only above 12,000 feet in South America.

Some species have a wide distribution. The American Avocet nests from Alberta to southern Texas and winters to Guatemala. The Black-winged Stilt nests in central Europe and Asia. One species, the Banded Stilt, lives only in patches of the southern half of Australia. It feeds in salt lakes, principally on brine shrimp. I once saw some 10,000 feeding while swimming on a settling pond at a huge salt works near Adelaide — the whole surface was dotted with black and white birds.

Painted Snipe (*Rostratula benghalensis*)   There are only two members of the
family of painted snipes. This one is found in Africa, Asia and Australia. It is
rail-like in that the wings are rounded, and the legs dangle when it flies. It is
one of the few birds whose female (shown here) is the more strongly
marked, and does not participate in the incubation or care of the young.

Red Knot (*Calidris canutus*)   The attractive brick coloring shown here disappears after the nesting season, and the feathering becomes nondescript. This chunky ten-inch sandpiper has almost worldwide distribution. It feeds in large flocks, usually mixed with other shorebirds.

Right: Greater Yellowlegs (*Tringa melanoleucus*)   Both the Greater and Lesser Yellowlegs are western hemisphere species which nest from Alaska to the Canadian prairies, and winter from the coasts of the United States to Argentina. They are noisy birds, uttering their descending *tew, tew, tew* calls as they take off from marsh or shore.

Lesser Yellowlegs (*Tringa flavipes*)   The two yellowlegs species can only be distinguished by size (14 inches and 10 inches) and by their calls. The Lesser's call is not as strident and is usually repeated more often. The bright yellow legs are diagnostic.

Right: Willet (*Catoptrophorus semipalmatus*)   The bird shown here is in a typical posture and location, for it often perches on posts in marshes. The strongly marked wings identify this large, stout-billed sandpiper in flight. It nests on the coasts and central plains of North America and winters from New Jersey and Washington south to Chile.

Marbled Godwit (*Limosa fedoa*) This large sandpiper nests only as far north as the prairies of Canada. It is rare in the east, and winters on the West Coast, in the Caribbean and south to Chile. In Audubon's time, the mid-nineteenth century, the large migration in the east was gradually destroyed by heavy shooting.

Pectoral Sandpiper (*Calidris melanotos*)   Found in Siberia and the northern shores of North America, this sandpiper winters in South America and Japan. It is seen in the United States and southern Canada only on migration. It is identified by its yellowish legs and brown-streaked breast.

Common Snipe (*Capella gallinago*) With almost worldwide distribution, this is one of the best known of birds. During nesting it has a wonderfully erratic flight which consists of zigzagging over its mate. It is at this time that the tail feathers rattle together, giving a strange chittering sound.

Right: Dunlin (*Calidris alpina*) This photograph was taken in the spring when the bird wore its black belly patch. Dunlins are circumpolar, nesting high in the Arctic, and wintering to Mexico, Africa and India. On migration they may be found in wet fields, probing for grubs and worms, but in winter they are found only on the coasts.

Least Sandpiper (*Calidris minutilla*)   This is the smallest of the North American sandpipers which, despite its modest six inches, travels vast distances, sometimes from Alaska to Chile and back. It is seen in flocks on migration along the coast and inland in North America, running about on the sand snapping up insects for fuel, almost always in the company of other shorebirds.

Whimbrel (*Numenius phaeopus*)   This large sandpiper nests around the
northern part of the globe in disjunctive patches and winters to South
Africa and Tasmania. It may be seen on migration flying along in lines or in
vees. Apart from the usual diet of crabs and mollusks, it also takes fruit and
berries.

Left: Long-billed Curlew (*Numenius americanus*) The largest of the North American sandpipers, this curlew nests from the southern prairies of Canada through the American west. It migrates no farther than Guatemala. The long bill can be seen here against the sky. It nests inland, but winters mostly on the coast.

Stilt Sandpiper (*Calidris himantopus*) Out of the nesting season the Stilt Sandpiper loses the chestnut eye stripe apparent here. It nests in the northern tundra of North America, and winters from the extreme southern United States to South America. It usually feeds while wading at belly depth, probing the bottom in a methodical manner.

American Woodcock (*Philohela minor*)   The only North American woodcock,
it lives permanently in the eastern half of the United States and Canada
where it remains classified as a game bird. Its spectacular mating flight takes
place at dusk — the male circling high, then plunging to earth on a
zigzagging course.

Western Sandpiper (*Calidris mauri*) The small sandpipers are much alike, particularly in winter before they grow their breeding plumage. This one is full plumaged, showing the rich brown typical of this species. It nests principally on the north coast of Alaska, but is often seen in the east on migration in North America.

Left: American Avocet (*Recurvirostra americana*) There are four species of avocets, this being the only one in the western hemisphere. It is a delicate-looking shorebird with a thin upswept bill, strongly marked black and white body, and cinnamon head and neck. The bill sweeps back and forth in the water as it gathers in tiny larvae.

Red Knot (*Calidris canutus*) The knot nests near fresh water marshes in the Arctic tundra, but prefers a coastal habitat extending from the Mediterranean and the Caribbean to the end of land in the south. It feeds in mud, but seems to favor rocky outcrops and pebble beaches.

White-rumped Sandpiper (*Calidris fuscicollis*)   This abundant little
sandpiper nests principally in the Arctic Islands of North America and
winters as far south as the Strait of Magellan. It is commonly seen on
migrations on the Atlantic coast and inland, but decreasingly farther west.

Baird's Sandpiper (*Calidris bairdii*)   This bird nests across the islands and mainland between Greenland in the east to Siberia, and migrates to Argentina, mostly through western North America. In Chile many spend the winter in mountains up to 13,000 feet, where they feed on insects and crustacea.

Wood Sandpiper (*Tringa glareola*)   Unlike most shorebirds, this Old World sandpiper perches readily in trees and on posts, particularly during the nesting season. It breeds across northern Europe and Asia and migrates to Asia, Australia and Africa. When flushed it towers quite high before going on its way.

Right: Hudsonian Godwit (*Limosa haemastica*)   At one time it was thought that this large sandpiper was becoming extinct. Their patchy nesting areas were little known, and they were seldom seen on migration. It was determined that they took off from the shores of Hudson's Bay and flew over settled areas, taking the long sea route to South America. Numbers appear to be stable or improving.

Short-billed Dowitcher (*Limnodromus griseus*)   Dowitchers feed principally
on marine and clam worms when on the coast. In all areas they drive their
bills deep in the soft mud and feel for their food. Small snails and mollusks,
as well as insect larvae, are part of their diet.

Black-winged Stilt (*Himantopus himantopus*) This stilt normally wades in shallow water to feed, but, on occasion, great numbers will congregate on a saline pond and swim, snapping up emerging brine flies. They nest in colonies close to water.

Spotted Sandpiper (*Actitis macularia*) This is the best-known sandpiper in North America, for it nests all over the continent, along streams, on ponds, and in marshes. It feeds along the edge of the water, hopping over branches and roots. In flight it flutters along, appearing to use only the tips of the wings.

STORKS

Wood Stork (*Mycteria americana*)   The Wood Stork nests in large colonies from the southern United States to Argentina and Peru. In Florida many of its habitat and feeding areas have been destroyed by drainage for crops and housing.

Many people gain their first impression of storks from greeting cards of congratulations upon the birth of a baby, or from advertisements for diaper services. The fantasy that storks deliver babies to households originated in Austria and Germany centuries ago, largely because of the White Stork's tendency to nest near human habitation. This is the bird whose large nest is seen perched on prominent buildings in many parts of Europe, sometimes in groups, but more often nowadays with only a single pair per village, if there are any at all. The White Stork has been a symbol of continuity in Europe and the Near East since biblical times because it returns year after year to the same nest site — some church spires having been occupied every summer for centuries. While most stork species are relatively sedentary, moving only in search of the rain that multiplies their food supply, the White Stork is not typical, for it migrates northward into Europe and central Asia from its wintering areas in Africa and southern Asia in the spring.

There are some 17 species of storks, as well as the Hammerkop and the Whale-headed Stork, both of Africa, which are of other families. All prefer tropical or sub-tropical areas in which to live. The Americas have only three species — the Maguari of South America, the giant Jabiru, which lives intermittently from Mexico to Argentina, and the American Wood Stork, which is the only one nesting as far north as the southern United States. The rest are widely distributed on both sides of the equator as far east as Japan and the northern half of Australia. They are large long-legged birds ranging in weight from 4 to 20 pounds, and standing from 30 to 60 inches in height. They have long pointed bills, thick and strong for prying open mollusks and snails. Most bills are straight, and that of the Wood Stork turns down.

The status of several species is precarious. The American Wood Stork, for instance, continues to do well in South America, but its population in the United States is decreasing rapidly. Its numbers there are concentrated principally in the Florida Everglades, where drainage for agriculture and recreational development has rapidly reduced the potential for feeding. In the center of the state enormous areas have been taken over for citrus, tomato, and subsidized sugar cane. All are saturated with chemicals which reduce the food supply to such an extent that nesting results are poor.

Census figures for the White Stork, accurate because of its visibility in Europe, have been maintained for longer than for any other bird. Its population has declined by a distressing 92 percent since 1900. The causes appear to be diverse — modern farming and insecticides have reduced food supplies, summers have become wetter, leading to fewer young surviving, and more and more birds are shot during the winter in Africa. During the present century, White Storks have disappeared entirely from Switzerland and Sweden, and elsewhere are in constant decline. The Milky Stork of southeast Asia, which nests in mangrove swamps, is in decline because of habitat destruction.

Some stork species find their food — a wide range of mollusks, frogs, larvae, fish, and worms — at water margins. Others take insects on savannahs. The White Stork is known in Africa as the grasshopper bird, from its habit of following the locust swarms. On the African plains some species, particularly the forbidding-looking Marabou, join the various vultures at a carcass after the original predator has taken its fill. I have seen as many as six species of storks and a number of vultures competing with hyenas at the same carcass. The Greater Adjutant Stork, which was once common in the cities of India, had the gruesome habit of cleaning up unwanted human remains.

The feathers of storks are, for the most part, in patterns of white, gray and black. Immature White Storks are pure white, later growing black feathers in their wings. Bill colors vary, in most species intensifying during the nesting season. The Saddle-billed has a scarlet tip and base with a wide black band in the middle. It also has bright red knee joints. The Painted Stork, which I saw in Sri Lanka, has a mustard-colored bill and bald head, black streaks on the white wings and a lovely crimson streak on both sides of the back. Asia and Africa each have their own species of open-billed stork, the bill having a noticeably wide gap between the tip and the base. Two species, the Greater Adjutant and the Marabou, have grotesque red air sacs hanging from the neck.

Nesting is varied. Some species nest colonially, others singly. Wood Storks in South America may have colonies of tens of thousands of birds. Some nest during the dry season, some in the wet depending upon the availability of food. Most lay from three to five eggs, the Saddle-billed only one. Incubation varies from 30 to 50 days with fledging for some taking more than four months.

Their long broad wings make storks excellent soaring birds. Often in the middle of a sunny day they may be seen rising to great heights on thermals for an hour or so, returning to earth in a tumbling flight. Like ravens, they sometimes demonstrate their abilities in aerobatics, often turning over in flight.

Painted Stork (*Ibis leucocephalus*) Remarkably attractive, this stork has a distinctive streak of pink on its white back and flight feathers. It lives in India, Indochina and Sri Lanka where it feeds principally on frogs, snakes and insects while wading in shallow ponds.

Right: Saddle-billed Stork (*Ephippiorhynchus senegalensis*) This is the largest stork in East Africa, measuring up to five and a half feet. It is uncommon throughout its range, rare in Ethiopia and Kenya, but rather more plentiful in Uganda and Tanzania. It lives in pairs or in small family groups in swamps and at the edge of lakes.

Marabou Stork (*Leptoptilos crumeniferus*)   This is probably the most populous stork resident in East Africa. It lives principally by scavenging the kills of the hunting animals, congregating in large numbers with the vultures. It also feeds on frogs and is beneficial in its consumption of locusts. It is an eerie sight in the evening, lining the branches of an acacia.

Jabiru Stork (*Jabiru mycteria*)   This Central and South American stork
circles at great height at midday, dwarfing the Wood Storks with its huge
wingspan. It nests well up in large trees, usually standing alone. Its flight is
light for such a large bird.

White Stork (*Ciconia ciconia*) This is the stork which, according to European legend, brings babies. It nests on chimneys and steeples in Europe and migrates to Asia and Africa, mostly around the eastern end of the Mediterranean. The population has declined by 90 percent since 1900 due to changes in agriculture and climate.

Marabou Stork (*Leptoptilos crumeniferus*)   This is a typical evening sight on the African plains. Marabous sit huddled, their necks drawn in to the shoulder, ominous and almost prehistoric-looking. The perch tree is often shared by a number of species of storks and vultures.

Yellow-billed Stork (*Ibis ibis*)   This stately pair lives on inland waters and on the coast in East Africa. The Yellow-billed Stork nests in colonies with others of its species and is generally silent, although it utters harsh croaks when near its nest.

White-bellied or Abdim's Stork (*Sphenorhynchus abdimii*) This handsome stork walks like a peacock. It is really not a wading bird for it lives in the plains and desert country between Ethiopia and the Transvaal. It nests in the north end of this range and migrates to the south. It moves about in flocks of considerable size.

Hammerkop (*Scopus umbretta*) This strange-looking bird, somewhat resembling a duck, is the only member of its family. It builds a huge nest in the fork of a tree, usually over water. It feeds at the margins of water and often lives deep in papyrus swamps. It is uncommon everywhere in its range in central and eastern Africa.

PHOTOGRAPH CREDITS

Brian Beck, 25, 58, 140
Peter Bisset, 12, 93, 120, 127
Fred Bruemmer, 52, 70, 123, 125
Pauline Brunner, 33, 129
Victor Fazio, 23, 27, 53, 69, 71, 89
Peter Ginn, 24, 34, 44, 72, 94, 95, 138, 141, 142
Cy Hampson, 37, 48, 92, 112, 117
Edgar Jones, 100
Thomas Kitchin, 2, 8, 77, 96, 99
Aubrey Lang, 41, 101
Wayne Lynch, 21, 29, 60, 75, 79, 98, 110, 115, 119, 128, 137
Robert McCaw, 113, 116, 130
Brian Milne/First Light Associated Photographers, 108, 109
Nico Myburgh, 9, 26, 31, 51, 65, 78, 97, 102, 103, 107, 126
Network/Barry Griffiths, 13, 17, 33, 136
Will Nichol, 18, 22, 36, 55, 87, 88
Scott Nielsen, 83
James Page, 114, 118, 121
George Peck, 42, 43, 47, 59, 72, 73, 91, 93
Mark Peck, 19, 24, 35, 45, 46, 54, 74, 76, 90, 124
Barry Ranford, 49
James Richards, 131
Wilfried Schurig, 28, 111
Duane Sept, 20, 64, 134
Karl Sommerer, 61, 62
J.D. Taylor, 4-5, 30, 32, 63, 82, 122, 135, 141
Ron Watts/First Light Associated Photographers, 50, 139

Left: Hammerkop (*Scopus umbretta*)   This picture shows the great bulk of the Hammerkop's nest, here perched on a prominent rock. The nests are located singly and may be used, with refurbishing, year after year.

INDEX TO PHOTOGRAPHS